I0817594

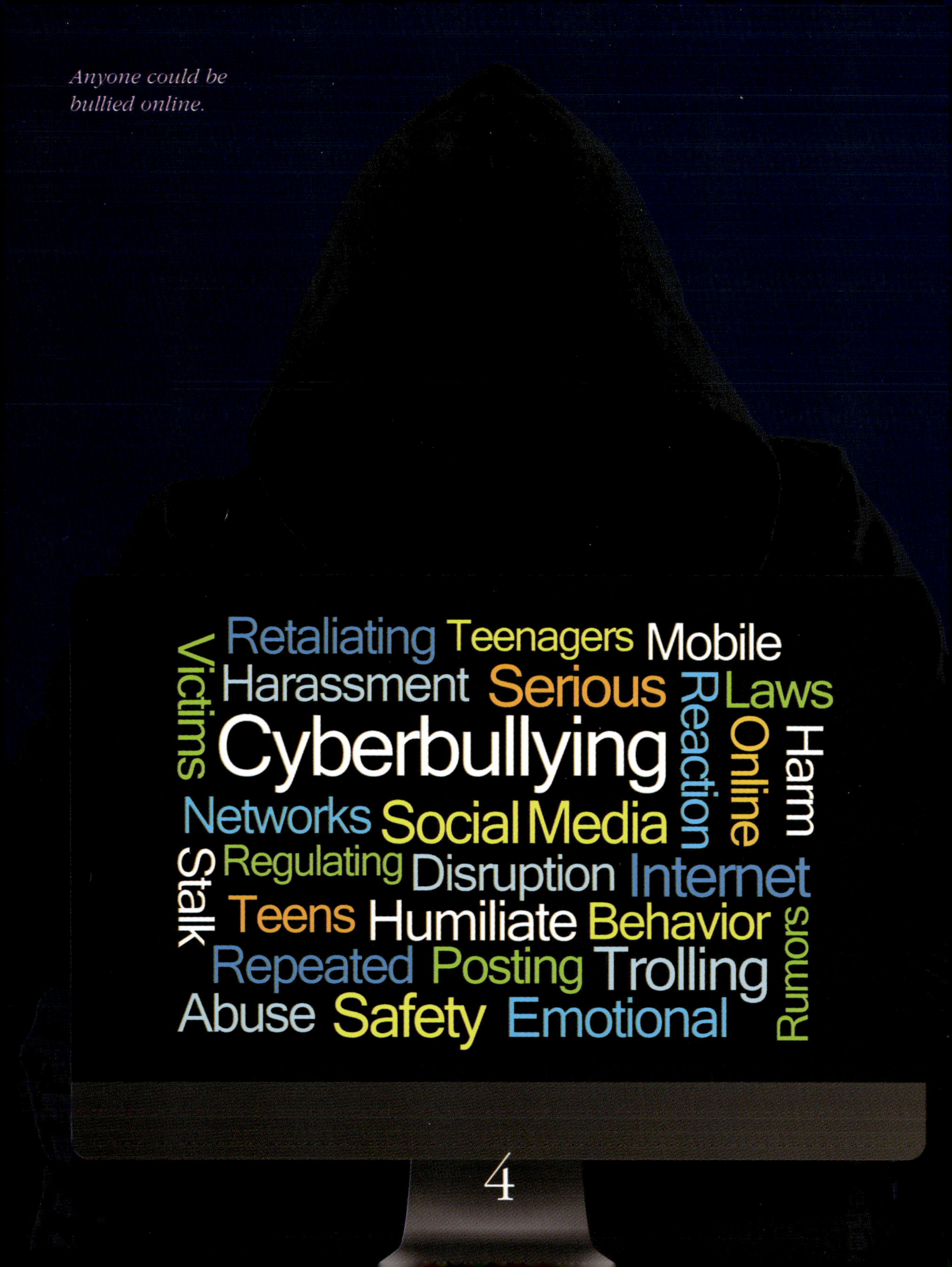

Anyone could be bullied online.

TECH SMARTS

12 QUESTIONS ABOUT CYBER BULLYING

BLACK RABBIT BOOKS

MARNE VENTURA

Table of Contents

What Is *Cyberbullying?*

1

Cyberbullying is a type of bullying. Bullying is action meant to make a person feel bad. It might make the victim feel **embarrassed** or sad. They may feel mad or afraid. Bullying often happens over and over. It usually happens in front of other people. Bullies might hit or shove their victims. Or bullies may tease or call them names.

Bullies attack in person. Cyberbullies attack online. They use texts, social media posts, and messages. Online attacks may be seen by more people than real-life attacks. Cyberbullies share mean messages about the target on social media. They text or email hurtful messages. They post embarrassing photos of the target. Both bullies and cyberbullies aim to hurt their targets.

Internet router

Cyberbullying can be more harmful than real-life bullying. In real life, avoiding a bully can help. But cyberbullying is harder to avoid. Online posts are almost impossible to erase completely. Texts and images are stored by websites. Other people might download and save them. They could take a screenshot and send it to others. For this reason, cyberbullying can feel like it will never end. But you can fight cyberbullying. You can get help.

Kids who are part of the LGBTQ+ community are more likely to be bullied.

22 Percent of students ages 12 to 18 who reported being bullied online or by text in 2022.

Bullies might threaten to hurt the target. • They might say unkind things about the way the target looks, acts, or dresses. • They might tell others not to be friends with the target.

THINK ABOUT IT

Do you think there should be rules about using technology to bully? What are some rules you think would be helpful?

Online bullying can make someone feel alone.

2 Who Is Involved in *Cyberbullying?*

Four types of people are involved in bullying. *Cyberbullies* use technology to embarrass or hurt other people. *Targets* are the people cyberbullies want to hurt. *Bystanders* are people who see bullying in action. They do not try to stop it. *Upstanders* are people who see bullying and try to stop it.

Bullying is a complex problem. People's roles can change. Bystanders can take sides. They can become upstanders by trying to stop the bullying. Or they can join the bully. Then they become bullies as well.

The people most hurt are the bullies and their targets. A bully's actions are often caused by problems in their lives. They might need help learning to control their feelings and actions. They might find it hard to follow rules. Targets often become sad or afraid. This

It is hard to know what someone is feeling or thinking behind a screen.

might lead to other unhealthy behaviors. But it is important to remember no two bullying situations are exactly alike. Bystanders and upstanders can be hurt by a bully's actions too.

Cyberbullying is often in the news. It might seem like it happens all the time. But it does not. Most kids are not bullies. It is not a normal behavior.

Targets may get direct messages from online bullies.

What Are the Effects of *Cyberbullying?*

3

Cyberbullying is an international public health concern. Many researchers are studying its effects. Cyberbullying is a threat to a teen's health and well-being. Many targets report higher feelings of **depression** and loneliness. They may get headaches and stomachaches. These are caused by **stress** and anxiety.

Targets can feel hopeless and powerless. They may have a harder time sleeping and focusing in class. Long-term bullying is connected to drug and alcohol use. The target may feel like no one cares. They just want everything to stop. Bullying victims are two to nine times more likely to have thoughts of suicide.

Even after the attacks stop, the target may be afraid. They may think the cyberbully will strike again. They may worry about all of the people who have read or seen the unkind posts. They may feel unsafe. This can lead to more problems. They might avoid school or events. They might lose interest in sports or hobbies. If you don't feel safe or are having thoughts of harming yourself, seek help right away. Start with a parent or teacher. These adults can become your **allies**. They can support you against cyberbullying.

93 Percent of targets who reported negative effects of cyberbullying.

School counselors, coaches, or religious leaders can be trusted adults. • Many teens see cyberbullying as normal. It is not. • Bystanders also may experience an increase in fear and anxiety.

Videos and photos make bullying worse.

THINK ABOUT IT

Imagine your friend has been the target of a cyberbully. What would you do to help them?

Are Bullies *Bad People?*

4

Cyberbullies don't just hurt their targets. Schools and communities are also harmed. Students might feel that their school or their community ignores bullying. This can make them feel unsafe. They might miss or even drop out of school. They might not want to join in school or community activities.

In those cases, it is easy to blame the bully. But it is important to look at the big picture. In some cases, the bully was first a target. This does not mean all targets become bullies. They don't. But kids who bully other kids have often been a target themselves. Bullying behavior is unkind. It is wrong. But kids often behave in ways that are wrong. Bad behavior does not make someone a bad person. It is possible for a bully's behavior online to follow them for the rest of their lives. Images, posts, and texts bullies

BRAIN RESEARCH The front part of your brain is called the prefrontal cortex. It helps control **impulses**. It helps you judge right from wrong. Research shows it does not fully develop until after the teen years. Sometimes young people make bad choices, like bullying. This could be because the brain is still developing.

A bully may be the victim of abuse at home.

share never go away completely. It might be possible to find them years after the bullying stops. Bullies might have a hard time making friends or finding a job, even if they no longer bully people.

It may feel good in the moment, but bullies may regret their choices.

Is It the Target's *Fault?*

5

No, bullying is never the target's fault. The blame lies with the bully. They choose actions that hurt other people. A cyberbully might send pictures of a party the target was not invited to. The bully hopes to make the target feel left out. The bully might know something that the target wants to keep private. Maybe they failed a test or didn't get picked for a sports team. The cyberbully might post this online. The bully hopes to embarrass the target. The bully might send cruel messages directly to the target. They might say "You're ugly," or "Nobody likes you."

Targets often do not ask for help. Sometimes, they feel ashamed. They think they have done something wrong. Sometimes, they are afraid. They worry the bullying will get worse if they tell. Targets might pretend bullying does not bother them.

It is important for targets to understand that they are not alone. Most of the time, talking with someone can help. Sometimes it helps to know others have been bullied too. It makes them feel less alone.

40 Percent of cyberbullying victims who report the problem to their parents.

Some targets worry they won't get to use the phone or computer if they report bullying. • Bullying can get worse if targets don't speak up. • Sometimes a school counselor or trusted teacher can help.

Bullies may send several mean messages in a row.

Cyberbullying could make a target fall behind in school.

Hanging out with friends or family is a good way to spend time away from social media.

TAKE A BREAK Ignoring bullies can be hard to do. It's also hard to give up your time on the phone or the computer. But taking a break from social media can help. Find other things to do. Learn to play an instrument. Go for a run. Read a good book. Hang out with friends in person. Taking breaks gives you time to think. You can figure out how to handle a bad situation without making it worse.

What Can Bystanders *Do to Help?*

6

Targets of bullies often feel ashamed or alone. This is because the attacks are often seen by other people. These people are called bystanders. They might see photos or unkind words shared by the cyberbully. Friends might show them messages that the bully sent.

Many bystanders do nothing. Some might be afraid they will become a target. Others may be friends with the bully. They might not think it is a big deal. But bystanders have the power to help. They can tell the bully to stop. They can choose not to share cruel posts. They can refuse to take part in the unkind actions.

Sometimes it can be unsafe for a bystander to speak up to the bully. The bully might try to harm the bystander. There are still ways the bystander can help. They can record what they see. They can print out the unkind posts. Then they can report the problem to a trusted adult. This might be a parent or teacher. When bystanders take action, they become upstanders.

87 Percent of bullying attacks seen by others.

Bystanders can tell targets they are on their side. • Bystanders can ask targets to join their group of friends. • Bystanders can be leaders by showing others how to help targets.

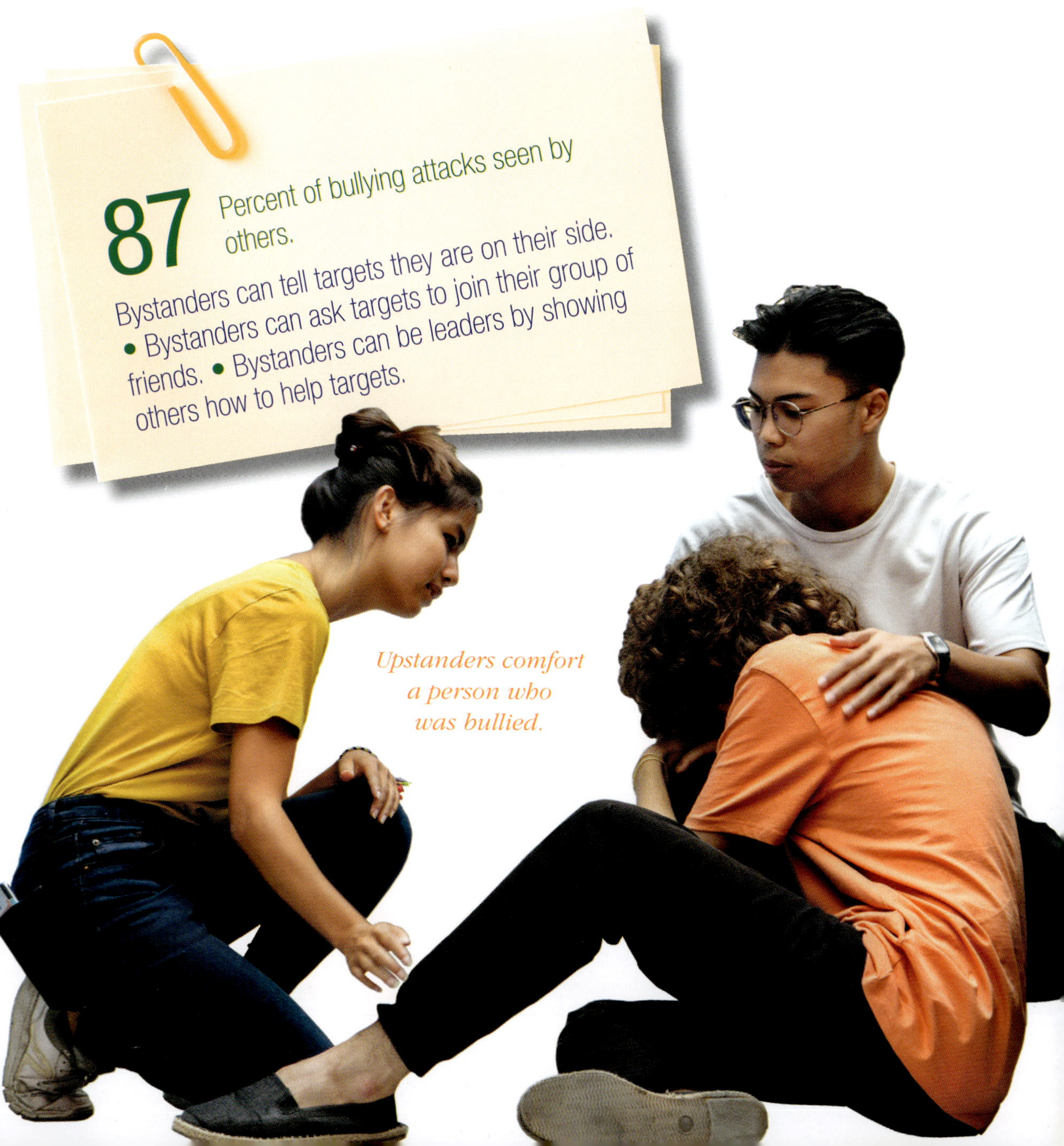

Upstanders comfort a person who was bullied.

SPEAK UP

It can be hard to stand up to a friend who is sending unkind messages to someone else. But if you do nothing, you are sending a message to the bully. You are telling them their actions are okay. Speak up against cyberbullies. If you see something, don't laugh or participate. Say something to an adult.

How Do Upstanders Improve *the Situation?*

7

Like bystanders, upstanders see bullying behavior. But upstanders choose to take action. Upstanders offer to help the target. They show the target he or she has friends who care. If they hear others spreading the bully's unkind words, they defend the target. They refuse to take part in the cruelty. They speak up about bullying. They say it is wrong.

Some schools have programs that teach students to be upstanders. They stress the importance of being kind to others. Students learn how to stand up to bullies in safe ways. They might practice by **role-playing**. They talk about their experiences with bullying. They think about ways to stop it in their communities.

As an upstander, you can do several things to help. If you see a cruel post or message, say something. If you

10 Number of seconds it takes to stop most bullying attacks after an upstander intervenes.

Research shows that when one person stands up, others follow. • Support from others can help targets feel less hurt by bullies. • Standing up can be hard, but stopping bullies is worth it.

Standing up against bullying can help others do the same.

feel safe, post a comment. You might say "This is not OK." You might post something nice about the target. If the bully posts a lie about the target, point that out. Do not laugh at the post or share it with your friends. Be a model for your classmates. Never share or post things online that would hurt someone else.

WORDS HAVE POWER

Bullies have been around for thousands of years. But cyberbullies are new. That's because the internet has only been around for a few decades. The word "upstander" was added to the *Oxford English Dictionary* in 2016. Two New Jersey high school students helped get the word added.

What Do Schools *Say?*

8

Cyberbullying often happens away from school. That's why schools have a hard time fighting it. But it often leads to in-person bullying at school. Then schools can step in. Rules about technology and computers can help stop cyberbullying at school.

School rules to prevent bullying vary from state to state. In New Jersey, principals must investigate all bullying. They must do it within a day after it is reported. They have 10 days to turn in a report to the school district. The report is then read at the next school board meeting. In Georgia, students who get caught bullying three times are taken out of regular school. They must go to an **alternative school**.

It can be hard to stop cyberbullying. But research shows schools can take steps to lessen it. First, schools should have ways for students to talk about

88 Percent of US school districts that have a cyberbullying prevention **policy**.

Teachers and school staff can learn the signs of cyberbullying. • Schools can have a safe space where victims can report bullies. • Schools can teach kindness and support upstanders.

cyberbullying. Schools need a system that lets students report bullies **anonymously**. This helps the upstanders feel safe. They know the bully will not strike back. Encouraging kindness on the school grounds can also stop cyberbullying.

A teacher can be a good ally against bullies.

What Does the Law *Say?*

9

All US states have anti-bullying laws. The specific laws vary from state to state. But they all ban bullying. According to the laws, schools must track and stop any bullying.

Almost all states also have laws against cyberbullying. In some states, cyberbullying is a crime. Officials sometimes disagree on which actions are cyberbullying. That's why it is important to keep a record of cyberbullying. You can do this by saving messages and photos or videos. Cyberbullying can include threats of violence. It can include pictures or videos of a person in a private place. In many cases, cyberbullies attack victims because they are different in some way. These cases should be reported to the police. They are considered **criminal** cyberbullying.

Don't be afraid to report bullying.

Sometimes it is hard to know the difference between teasing and bullying. Teasing can be a playful way to talk to others. You might tease your best friend for always bringing the same lunch to school. Your friend might tease you for wearing your favorite shirt so often. Bullying is different. A bully's goal is to hurt the target. These kinds of online posts are against the law.

THINK ABOUT IT

Think of a time when you were teased online. How did it make you feel? Could the teasing become bullying? With this in mind, do you think cyberbullying should be a crime?

Cyberbullying can be reported to law enforcement.

48 Number of US states with laws against cyberbullying.

Wisconsin and Alaska do not have laws against cyberbullying. • It is important to document and report any form of bullying. • In some states, cyberbullies can be removed from a classroom or expelled from school.

How Can Safe Online Behavior Prevent *Cyberbullying?*

10

Cyberbullying takes place through a computer, phone, tablet, or gaming console. It can be easy to forget there is a real person who reads the message. People often send messages that they would never say face-to-face. Once a message is sent, it cannot be taken back. Learn to be careful online. Help make social media safe.

Following some simple rules can help. Be kind to others. Respect the fact that people are different. If a classmate asks you to keep something private, don't share it. Think about your message before you send it. Stick to true, positive statements. Words that would hurt someone in real life hurt online too. Anything that would be wrong to say in person is wrong to say online.

It is never a target's fault for bullying. But there are ways you can protect yourself. First, think before you post online. Only share photos or videos you don't

PARENTAL CONTROL

13 Minimum age a person must be to join TikTok.

Experts say kids younger than 13 should limit social media time to 30 minutes per day. • There are social media sites made for kids younger than 13. • Kid-friendly apps offer safety features and require parent permission.

mind everyone seeing. Second, protect your password. Remember to log out of public computers at school and the library. Third, keep private information private. This helps protect your **identity**. It makes it more difficult for a bully to find you.

Lastly, use age-appropriate sites. There is a reason you must be a minimum age to join social media sites. Those rules exist to keep kids safe online.

Many kids are eager to start using social media sites.

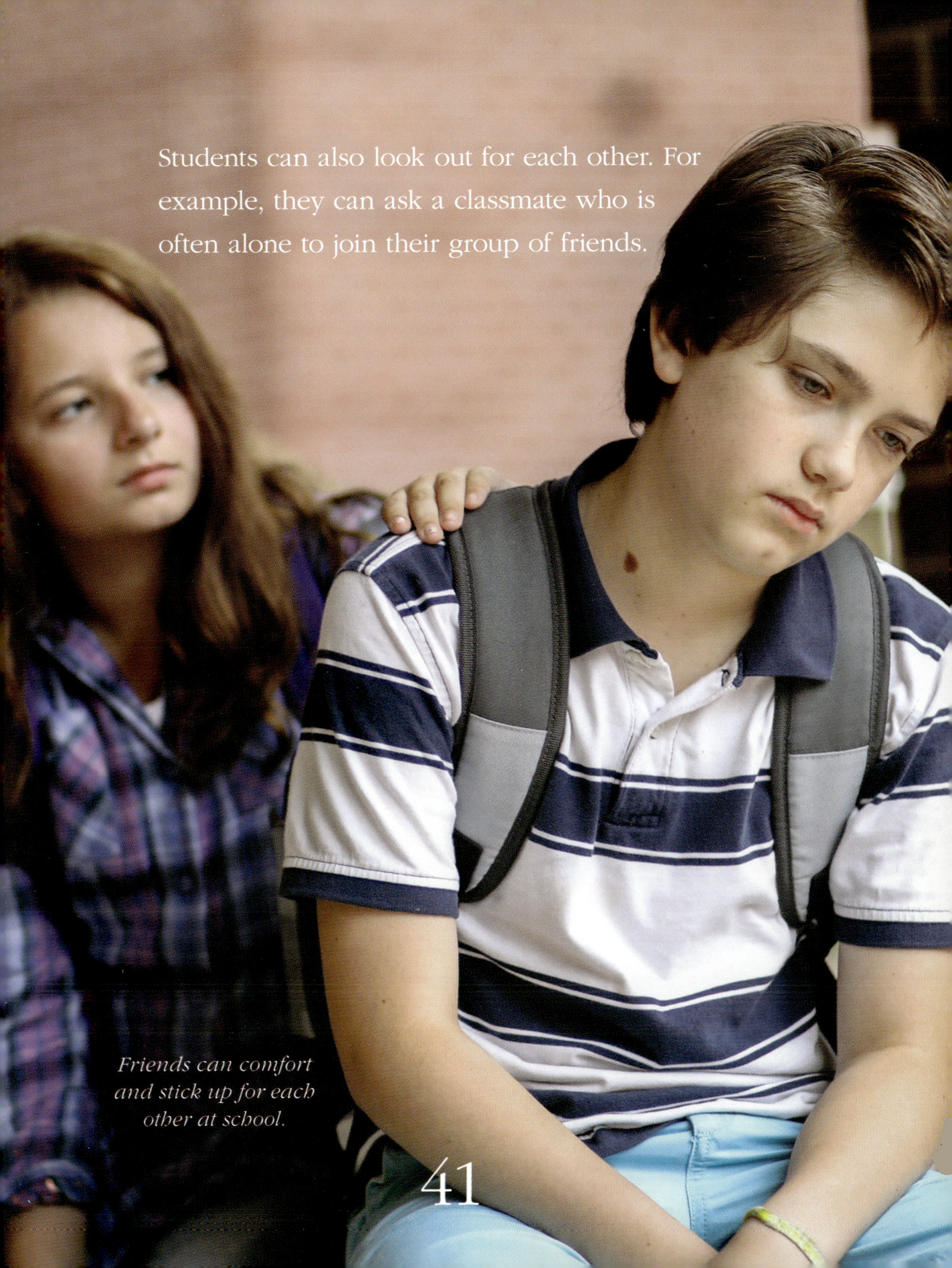

Students can also look out for each other. For example, they can ask a classmate who is often alone to join their group of friends.

Friends can comfort and stick up for each other at school.

Teens who use cell phones report a higher rate of cyberbullying.

POSITIVITY BALLOON One day, you might see a mean post about a classmate. You know this is wrong. Instead of ignoring the post, you share something positive about the target. You ask your friends to join. They write kind messages. Soon, everyone is seeing your posts. The positivity spreads. This is one way you can break the cycle. It takes away the bully's power to hurt with words.

Tips for Dealing

Make A Stand

Do not encourage bullying. Tell the bully to stop. Or find an adult who can do this. Do not share or "like" hurtful posts. If you see someone recording an embarrassing moment, say something. It is not okay to laugh at someone else's discomfort. You can be a leader for others to follow.

Block and Report

It is best to ignore a bully. This takes away their power. But this can be hard to do online. If you see something upsetting, take a break from being online. Don't respond or get even. Instead, block them. Speak to someone you trust about it. Bullying can get worse. It is important to report it.

with Cyberbullying

Offer Support

The target may feel alone or scared. Reach out in friendship. You can help them find help. Even if you are scared, you can help in private. It takes courage to stand up. If your friend is a bully, pull them aside. Tell them their behavior is not okay. Then offer help. They may be bullied themselves. You can help stop the cycle.

Find Help

Bullying can make victims feel sad and even depressed. This may be lead them to think about suicide. Most victims do not become suicidal. But if you are feeling hopeless, you can contact Lifeline. It is a suicide prevention site. Call or text 988 any time. Or visit 988lifeline.org to chat with someone.

Glossary

ally
A person or group that gives help to another person or group.

alternative school
A nontraditional learning environment for students who have been removed from the classroom due to poor behavior or wrongdoing.

anonymously
In a way that prevents a person from being known by name.

confront
To deal with something in an honest and direct way.

criminal
Involving illegal activity.

depression
A state of feeling very sad, hopeless, and unimportant to the point of being unable to live in a normal way.

embarrass
To make someone feel confused and foolish in front of others.

identity
Who someone is, including their real name, address, birthdate, and other personal information.

impulse
A sudden desire to do something.

intervene
To become involved in something in order to have an influence on what happens.

policy
An officially accepted set of rules or ideas about what should be done.

role-play
An activity in which people do and say things while pretending to be in a particular situation.

stress
The state of mental worry caused by problems in your life.

unfriend
To remove someone from a list of friends or contacts on a social media site.

For More Information

Books

Clark, Katie. *Dealing with Online Bullies*. Minneapolis: Lerner Publications, 2026.

Knabb, Muriel. *Teens Dealing with Online Bullying*. San Diego: BrightPoint Press, 2025.

Ventura, Marne. *12 Questions about Social Media*. Mankato, MN: Black Rabbit Books, 2025.

Websites

Cyberbullying
kidshealth.org/en/teens/cyberbullying.html

What Teens Can Do
www.stopbullying.gov/resources/teens

About the Author

Marne Ventura is the author of more than 150 books for children. A former elementary school teacher, she holds a master's degree in reading and language development from the University of California. Ventura's nonfiction titles cover a wide range of topics, including media literacy, STEM, arts and crafts, food and cooking, biographies, health, history, and survival. Ventura and her family live in California.

Index

TOP RANK is published by Black Rabbit Books, P.O. Box 227, Mankato, MN, 56002.

• Designed by Danny Nanos • Photographs © Dreamstime/Adonis1969, 30, 34, Anna Griessel, 28–29, Denisismagilov, 35, Pentex, 7, Prostockstudio, 2, 18, Rclassenlayouts, 44–45; Getty Images/fotosipsak, 36, fstop123, 41, Imgorthand, 20, Peter Dazeley, 17, 19, SolStock, 27, StockPlanets, 40, 42–43; Shutterstock/andriano.cz, 32–33, Belinda Pretorius, 48, BigTunaOnline, 38, Box Lab, 4, Daniel Hoz, 21, 22, Ermolaev Alexander, 9, Inside Creative House, 12, Jakkrit Orrasri, 44, Jolygon, 46–47, Ka Iki, 26, KieferPix, 45, Kotin, 13, Kunst Bilder, 37, leolintang, 2–3, 30–31, Linaimages, 10, MIA Studio, 5, New Africa, 39, NMK-Studio, 16, PeopleImages.com - Yuri A, cover, 1, 4, Pereslavtseva Katerina, 23, Rob Wilson, 4, Roman Bodnarchuk, 14, SB Arts Media, 7, surajet.l, 5, Tiko Aramyan, 15, Tint Media, 6, Viktoriia Hnatiuk, 8, 24, 25, XiXinXing, 38 • Printed in India

Library of Congress Cataloging-in-Publication Data: Names: Ventura, Marne, author. | Title: 12 questions about cyberbullying / by Marne Ventura. | Other titles: Twelve questions about cyberbullying | Description: Mankato, MN: Top Rank, an imprint of Black Rabbit Books, [2026] | Series: Tech smarts | Includes bibliographical references and index. | Preteens | Ages 9–13 | Grades 4–6 | Identifiers: LCCN 2024059061 (print) | LCCN 2024059062 (ebook) | ISBN 9781644668153 (library binding) | ISBN 9781644668474 (paperback) | ISBN 9781644668795 (ebook) | Subjects: LCSH: Cyberbullying—Juvenile literature. | Internet and children—Juvenile literature. | Classification: LCC HV6773.15.C92 V46 2026 (print) | LCC HV6773.15.C92 (ebook) | DDC 302.34/302854678—dc23/eng/20250118 | LC record available at https://lccn.loc.gov/2024059061